The Rubber Band Book

Everyone enjoys performing tricks to amaze their friends and constructing toys that really work. Among the many amusing projects in this book you will find puzzles and illusions, games to play and things to make – from a motorised steam engine to a harmless rapid repeater pistol and a greetings card that smiles! Created with ordinary rubber bands and cheap, everyday materials, the projects range from the very simple to the more complicated, providing hours of fun for children of all ages.

Eric Kenneway has written a number of books on crafts and origami.

D0179889

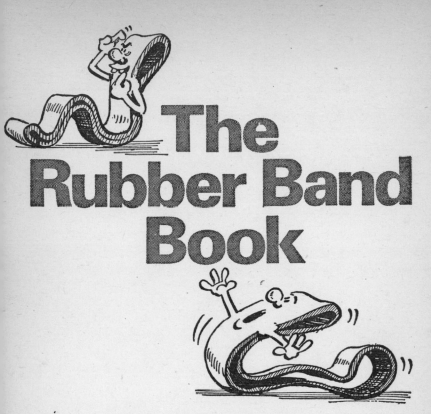

The Rubber Band Book

Eric Kenneway

Illustrated by Alan Rogers

Beaver Books

First published in 1977 by
The Hamlyn Publishing Group Limited
London · New York · Sydney · Toronto
Astronaut House, Feltham, Middlesex, England

© Copyright Text Eric Kenneway 1977
© Copyright Illustrations
The Hamlyn Publishing Group Limited 1977
ISBN 0 600 38753 4

Printed in England by Cox & Wyman Limited,
London, Reading and Fakenham
Set in Monotype Univers

FOREWORD

In the following pages you will find all sorts of tricks, stunts, games and other enjoyable things to do with rubber bands. If you have a rubber band ready, you can start right away on some of the projects in Part 1 ; for this section is made up of things to do using rubber bands and nothing else.

Part 2 contains things to do using rubber bands with other odds and ends. You will need to collect a few empty matchboxes, one or two clothes pegs and things of that sort. None of these required objects should be difficult to find.

Part 3 contains instructions for making things which need, in addition to rubber bands, material such as balsa wood. There are also one or two projects here which do not require any special craft material but do require a certain amount of accurate measuring. So most of the things which are quick and easy to do appear at the front of the book, while Part 3 contains the things which may take a little more time as well as more material.

Before you start

The things you need are listed at the beginning of every project. You will find rubber bands described as 'thin', 'long', 'wide' and so on. These descriptions are meant to be a rough guide only. Experiment with whatever rubber bands you have while you build up a collection of bands of different sizes for future use.

Further reading

There are many craft books which contain some projects in which rubber bands are used, but little is published about rubber bands in particular. *Investigating Science With Rubber Bands*, by Laurence B. White, Jr. published by Addison-Wesley Publishing Co, Reading, Mass, U.S.A. (1969), however, contains a lot of facts and many interesting ideas that rubber band enthusiasts will enjoy.

The 'Encyclopedia of Impromptu Tricks', by Martin Gardner, was published as a series of articles in *Hugard's Magic Monthly* beginning in the issue for March, 1951, and continuing for several years. It contains a large section on tricks with rubber bands, some of which appear in this book. It is a pity that this encyclopedia has never been published in book form and remains difficult for most people to find.

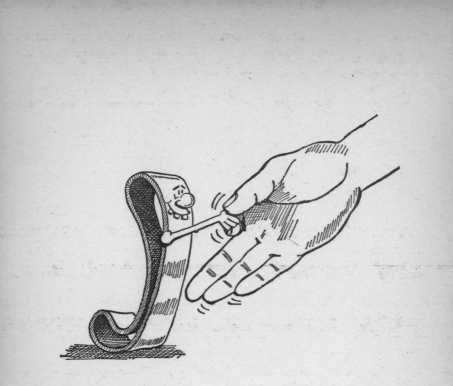

Thanks
Finally, it remains for me to thank Ray Bolt, Steve Carter, Mick Guy, Elsie Hill, Francis Martin, Lynn Merchant and Sam Randlett, who have all contributed in one way or another to making this little collection.

PART 1

THINGS TO DO
USING RUBBER BANDS
ONLY

Rubber band wrestling

This is a game for two people.

You will need : *one or more medium-sized rubber bands*

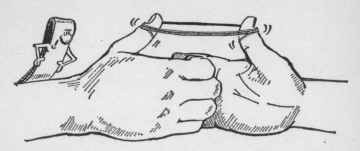

1.   Sit at a table facing each other. Each rest your right hand on the table ; hook your fingers together and keep your thumb raised. Place a rubber band around the two thumbs. (If there is a third person present, let him put the band in position and generally act as referee.)

2.   At the command : 'Go', try to capture the rubber band by wriggling it on to your own thumb without dropping it.
The rules can be varied. You may decide that the one who has won most often in a set of five or ten contests is the winner, or each contest may be treated separately – the winner takes the rubber band.

Shooting a rubber band

This is a very simple trick, but it is great fun to perform.

You will need: *one thin rubber band*

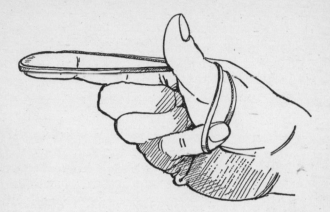

1.   Place one end of the rubber band round the tip of your forefinger, stretch it around your thumb and down, holding the other end in place with your little finger.

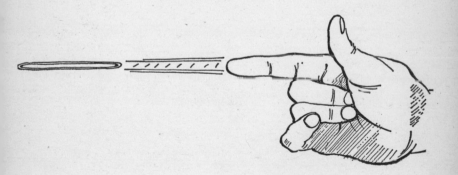

2.   Point at a target and raise your little finger. The band will be released and shoot towards whatever you are aiming at.

Jumping band

You will need: *one thin or medium-sized rubber band*

1. Place the rubber band on your forefinger.
2. Take hold of it with your other hand and pull it up behind your middle finger.

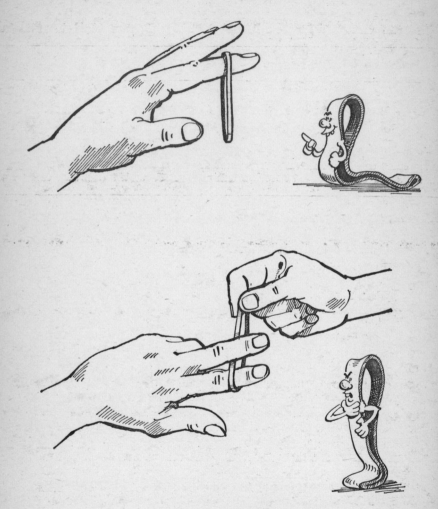

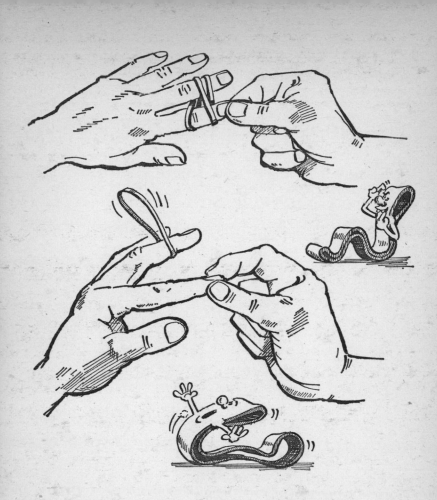

3.   Carry it over the middle finger and loop it on to the forefinger once more.

Now tell everybody that you will make the band jump from your forefinger to your middle finger. Ask somebody to hold the tip of your forefinger. This will make the trick look more difficult than it really is.

4.   Say, 'One . . . two . . . three . . . jump!' and quickly bend your middle finger. Part of the band will slip off which has the effect of releasing it entirely from the forefinger. The band will jump across and hang from the middle finger alone.

Twisted band
You will need: *one wide rubber band*

1.   Hold the band as shown with your right hand at the top and your left hand below. Give the band precisely two twists by running your right forefinger back against the thumb.

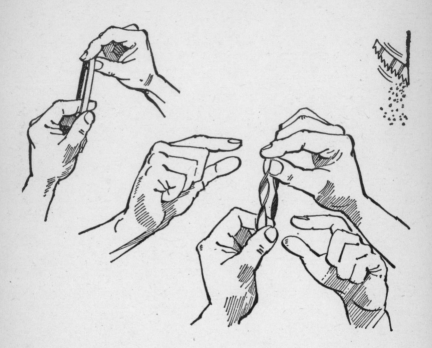

2.   Ask a friend to take the band from you. Make sure that he holds it in the same way that you are holding it, with the right thumb and finger at the top and the left thumb and finger at the bottom.

Now challenge him to remove the twists from the band. He must continue to grip each end firmly between thumb and finger, but apart from that may move his hands in any way he likes. He should find it impossible to remove the twists. ·

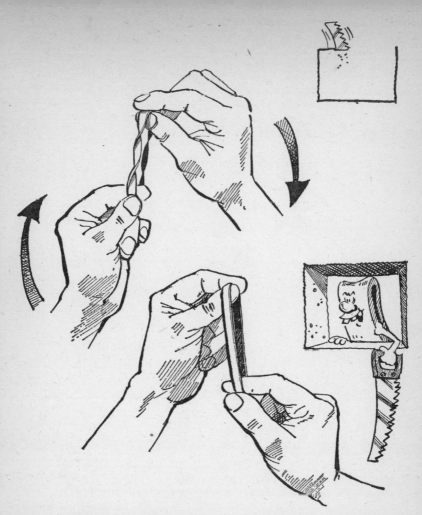

3.   Carefully take hold of the rubber band once more, holding it in the same way you did before. Show how easy it is by just moving your hands in a vertical circling motion; bring the left hand up and the right hand down . . .

4.   . . . and the twists have vanished. Your friend will wonder why he failed. Actually it is because he only appeared to be holding the band in the same way you were. In fact, because he took the band from the other side, his twists were the reverse of yours – and that makes all the difference.

15

Escaping band

You will need : *one medium-sized rubber band*

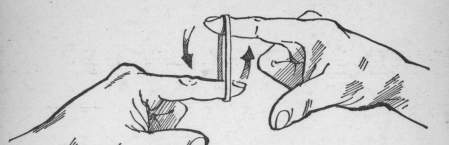

1. Place the forefinger of each hand into the loop of the rubber band and move your fingers in a circle away from you.

2. Bring the thumb tip and the tip of the forefinger of each hand together.

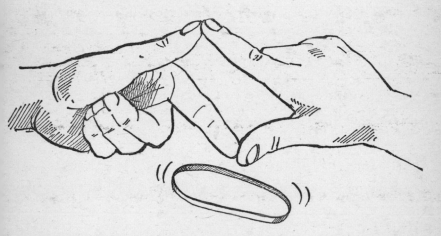

3. Switch fingertips so that
the right forefinger touches
your left thumb and vice versa.

4. Keeping the tips together, separate the thumb and fingers to
allow the rubber band to drop to the table.
When you are familiar with this little routine, run through it for
a friend and challenge him to do the same. He will probably find
that his rubber band becomes trapped around his fingers when
he reaches what should be the final step.

  This is because step 2 is not quite so straightforward as it
seems. You must have your fingers and the rubber band both
correctly placed when making this step. Be sure to follow the
illustration exactly.

Buttonhole illusion

You will need: *one long rubber band*
one buttonhole (so wear a jacket
or cardigan)

To be effective, this illusion needs to be performed in one fluid movement. Practise the following few steps until you are familiar with them. Then work up your speed before trying it on your friends.

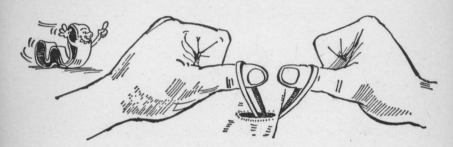

1. Pass the rubber band through your buttonhole. Place your thumbs through each end, bringing the thumb tips together.

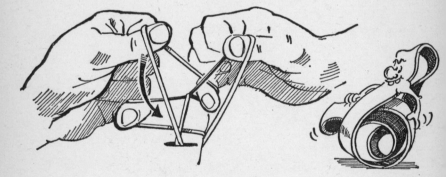

2. Hook your left little finger around the lower right side of the band. Hook your right little finger around the lower left side of the band. Then withdraw your left finger, bringing your left thumb down to hold the loop in position.

3. Withdraw your right little finger from its original loop . . .

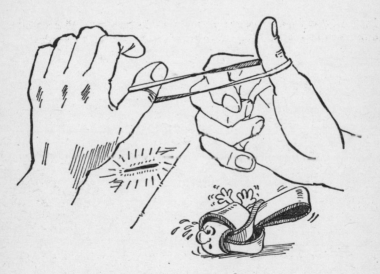

4. . . . and the rubber band is released from the buttonhole, apparently penetrating your jacket.

Another jumping band

You will need : *two rubber bands—one thin and one small*

1. Place the smaller band across the third and fourth fingers of one hand. Wind the thin band around your fingertips. (This is not essential but it makes the trick look more difficult.)

2. Bring your thumb across, hook the smaller band on to your thumbtip and stretch it back. Bend all four fingers forward into the band. Do this in one secret movement as you pass your other hand in front. Extend the fingers once more ...

3. . . . and the band has jumped on to the first and second fingers.

4. You can take the band back to the position illustrated in step 1 by pushing the band with the thumb of your other hand as you pass it across the palm.

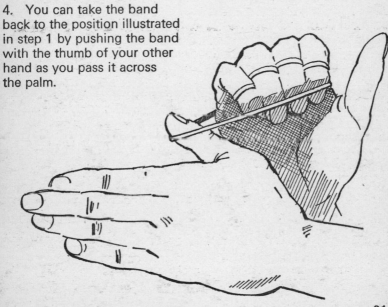

Penetrating bands

You will need: *two medium-sized rubber bands*

Note: In the illustrations the bands are made to appear differently coloured so that they can be distinguished more easily, but when actually performing this trick you should use ones of similar colour.

1. To start, stretch a band between the thumb and middle finger of your right hand. Hang the other band from your left thumb. Lower this band behind the first one and take the end on your left forefinger.

2. Slide one band along the other a few times, moving it back and forth in the direction of the arrows.

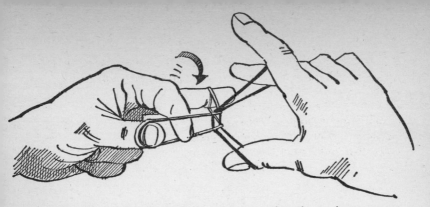

3.   In this step we secretly untrap the two bands so that we can create an illusion of penetration. Your right hand will hide what you do.

First place your left middle fingertip behind your left forefinger to hold that end of the band in position. Pull your right hand back, stretching the band. Bring the fore- and middle fingers of the left hand round to the front of the black band, meanwhile slipping the middle finger out of the white band which will automatically jump back on to the forefinger. Return to the position illustrated in fig. 2 (except that the white band is now in front of the black one).

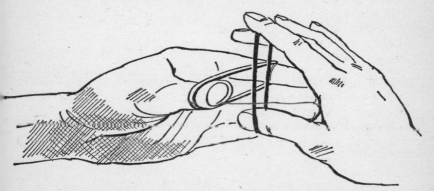

4.   Continue to slide the rubber bands together as if they were still trapped. (In fact, your audience should be unaware that step 3 has taken place.) Then say, 'I think I can feel it coming through now.' After a while, stop the sliding motion and separate the two bands with a sudden movement as if one had just cut right through the other.

Disappearing band

You will need: *one medium-sized rubber band*

It is a good idea to perform this trick immediately after completing the 'Penetrating Bands' when your audience has just seen you handling *two* rubber bands. Set up the trick by doing steps 1–3 casually with the hands under the table, or hidden in some other way.

1. Hang the rubber band on your right forefinger; give it a half twist and hook the other end on to your thumb.

2. Put your left thumb and forefinger through the two spaces as shown.

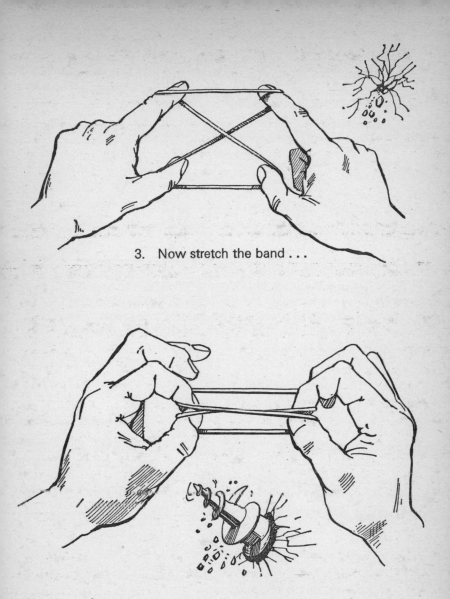

3. Now stretch the band . . .

4. . . . and bring your thumbs and fingertips together. At this point, bring your hands from under the table and show your audience what appears to be two rubber bands.

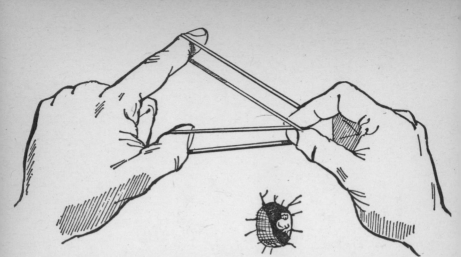

5. To increase the illusion that you are holding two bands, separate the thumb and forefinger of one hand, then close them again. Do the same with the other hand, keeping the thumb and forefinger of the first hand closed. Repeat these moves a few times, always remembering to keep the rubber band at full stretch.

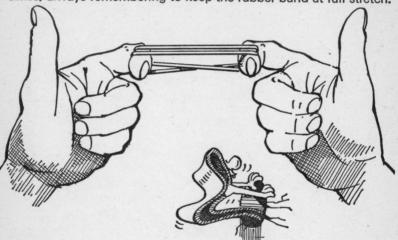

6. Bring your hands back to the position shown in step 4. Then slip the tips of your forefingers forward through both loops, releasing your thumbs. Do not relax the band; keep it stretched as you do this.

7.   Close your hands and rub the palms together. This releases the band from your fingers.

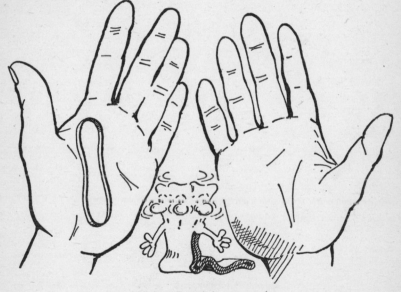

8.   With a flourish, open the left hand to reveal one rubber band. Open the other hand to reveal – nothing.

Making a rubber band chain

You will need: *lots of rubber bands*

1. Place one rubber band over another. Take the overlapped band by one end and pull it through itself.
2. Continue in the same way until the chain is as long as you want it and then knot the ends together.

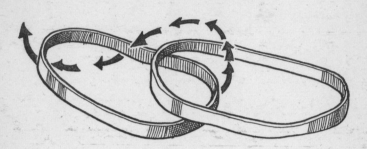

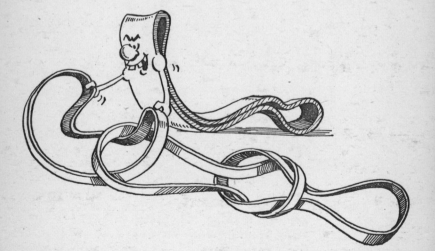

Rubber band necklace

One way of keeping your collection of rubber bands is to wear it as a chain around your neck.

Rubber band earring

Some rubber bands are brightly coloured. Join one of these to a thin band, and loop it over your ear to make an earring.

Chinese skipping
You will need: *lots and lots of rubber bands*

This is a jumping game – a test of skill – played by three or more people. First of all make a chain of rubber bands as shown on page 28. Knot the ends together to make a circle something over a metre in diameter.

  Two people stand facing each other about 2.5 metres apart with the loop of rubber bands around their ankles. The third person then starts the series of jumps as follows:

1. Starting position. (These illustrations always show the position at the start of each step.) Jump on to the near side of the loop.

2. Jump back.

3. Jump on to the far side of the loop.

4. Jump back again.

5. Jump over the far side of the loop, carrying the near side on top of the feet.

6. Jump and turn to one side.

7. Jump up to release the ankles and land straddling one side of the loop.

8. Jump to the side and straddle the other side of the loop.

9. Jump and turn to face the loop from the outside.

10. Jump over the far side, carrying the near side on top of the feet.

11. Jump and turn to one side.

12. Jump up to release the ankles and land straddling both sides of the loop.

13. Jump about turn, carrying one side of the loop on the toes of the right foot and the other side on the heel of the left foot.

14. Jump up to release the ankles and land inside the loop.

15. Jump out of the loop.

16. Finishing position.

On completing the series, or when failing at a jump, the jumper changes places with one of the people who have been standing at the sides.

When everybody has had a go, move the loop up to calf height and repeat all the steps. Then move the loop up to the knees; then up to the thighs and so on, as far as you can go without tying yourself in knots!

PART 2

THINGS TO MAKE
USING RUBBER BANDS
AND SCRAP

Banjo

You will need : *one thin rubber band*
one ruler
one empty matchbox

1. Stretch the rubber band
over the ruler; then place the
inside part of a matchbox
between the ruler and the
band. Slide it down as far as it
will go towards one end.

2. While plucking with the
thumb of one hand, place each
fingertip of the other hand on
the rubber band in turn. This
will shorten or lengthen the
'string' producing a higher or
lower note.
See if you can play a tune on
your banjo.

Clothes peg gun

You will need : *one medium-sized rubber band*
one sprung clothes peg
cotton wool buds

1. Place the rubber band around the length of the clothes peg.
Put a cotton wool bud into the mouth of the clothes peg,
pushing the end of the rubber band in with it.
2. To fire, just squeeze the clothes peg gently as if to open it.

Matchbox gun

You will need:
one medium-sized rubber band
one empty matchbox
one clothes peg
cotton wool buds

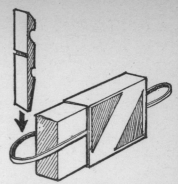

1. Remove the match tray from its outer part. Place the rubber band around the tray and replace it.

Break the clothes peg into two parts – you will only need one part. Insert this, flat side outwards, between the matchbox and the rubber band. Pull the rubber band tight so that the peg will stay in place.

2. Ready for loading: place half a cotton wool bud between the clothes peg and the box. Push it well down so that its head just shows.

3. Pull the front end of the rubber band back and loop it over the head of the cotton wool bud. Aim and fire by pressing the bottom end of the clothes peg with your thumb. The cotton wool bud will shoot across the room.

Flutterbug

You will need : *one thin rubber band*
paper (about 10 x 15cm)
glue

1. Divide the paper into two rectangles measuring about 7.5×10cm. Roll them tightly to make two firm cylinders.

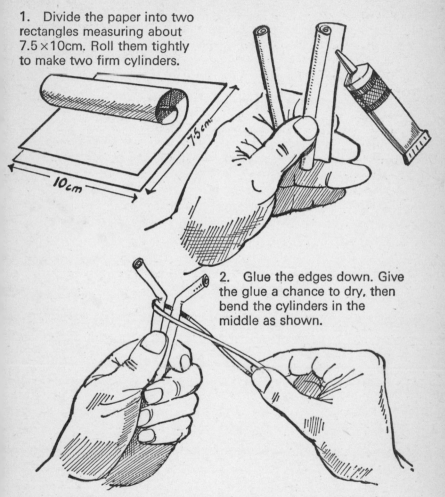

2. Glue the edges down. Give the glue a chance to dry, then bend the cylinders in the middle as shown.

3. Twist the rubber band several times around the middle of the cylinders.

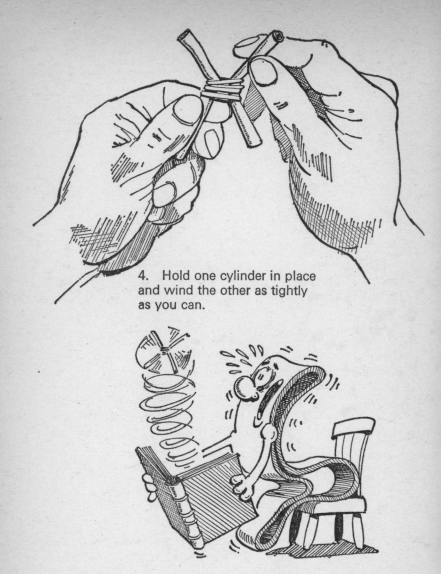

4. Hold one cylinder in place and wind the other as tightly as you can.

5. Hide the flutterbug by placing it between the pages of a book, or under a plate, or in some other place where it will soon be found. When the unsuspecting victim comes along and releases it, the flutterbug will fly up making a loud rattling noise.

Matchstick illusion
You will need: *one thin rubber band*
two matchsticks

Cut the heads from the two matchsticks. We do this not only to be safe but because the illusion will only be successful if the matchsticks are similar at both ends.

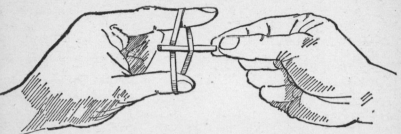

1. Place the rubber band around your thumb and forefinger. Put one matchstick into the loop and wind it up.

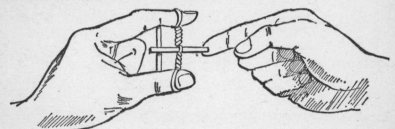

2. Place the other matchstick between thumb and forefinger as shown and rest one end of the wound-up matchstick against it.

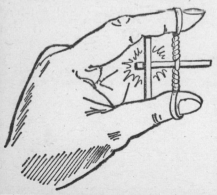

3. When the first matchstick is released, it will appear to slice through the other. The matchstick really travels the long way round, but it does it so quickly that the eye is deceived.

'Mama'

You will need : *one wide rubber band*
one empty cotton reel
craft knife or scissors

1. Uncover the centre hole of the cotton reel by neatly cutting away the centre of the label at each side.

2. Place a wide rubber band around the reel ; twist it and bring the end back up again.

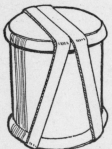

3. Arrange the two widths of the band so that they are stretched side by side, covering the hole at one end. The hole at the other end should be left uncovered.

4. Hold the uncovered end of the reel to your lips. Cup your hands around it and blow, opening and closing one hand. You will find that you can make the sound of a baby crying 'Mama'.

Hummer

You will need: *two or three large rubber bands*
a wire coat hanger
a piece of string

1. Pull down the cross wire of the coat hanger to make a frame for the rubber bands.

2. Stretch two or three untwisted rubber bands across the wire frame. Tie the string securely to the hook.

44

3. Hold the string and swing rapidly around in a circle. You will hear a humming noise as the rubber bands vibrate in the wind you create.
Be careful where you swing your hummer. It is better to use it outdoors, making sure nobody is standing close by.

Jack-in-the-box

You will need : *three thin rubber bands*
one empty matchbox
scrap of thin white card
fancy wrapping paper or
magazine cover
adhesive tape
craft knife or scissors
glue
pen or pencil

1. Remove the inside part of
the matchbox and cut two
round holes in its base as
shown.

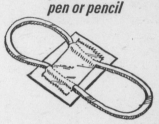

2. Cut the scrap of card into
a rectangle measuring about
2 × 2.5cm. Stick this to one of
the rubber bands with
adhesive tape.

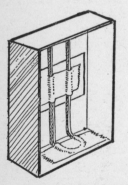

3. Now place this inside the
match tray so that the little
piece of card covers the two
holes. Stick the ends of the
rubber band to the inside of
the tray at top and bottom
with adhesive tape. Try to
keep the card in position as
you do so.

4. Turn the matchbox over
and make big dots in the
circles to form eyes.

5. Loop two rubber bands over the outer part of the matchbox. Push the inner part back into its casing until the slack has been taken up from the two bands.

6. From some fancy wrapping paper, or something similar, cut a strip about 5.5cm wide and at least 15cm long. Glue this around the matchbox casing.

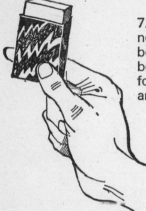

7. The Jack-in-the-box is now ready for use. Close the box and hold it firmly at the bottom between thumb and forefinger. Relax the pressure and Jack will pop up.

8. By placing the forefinger of the other hand against the little card, and moving it slightly, you can make Jack roll his eyes about.
When not in use, twist a rubber band around your Jack-in-the-box to keep it in the closed position.

Flying saucer

You will need:

one thin rubber band
one clothes peg
scrap of thin card
scissors or craft knife
bradawl
pencil and ruler

1. With the bradawl make a hole, top and bottom, about 1cm from the handling end of the clothes peg.

2. Thread the rubber band through both of the holes until it projects about equally above and below. Then take these two loops over and into the mouth of the clothes peg.

3. Now pull the rubber band tight to create a loop at the side. It is easier to do this if you use a matchstick or pin or something similar.

4. Draw a circle on the card. By drawing around a 10p piece you can make a circle of about 3cm diameter, which is big enough. A slightly bigger circle would be better still, but its diameter should not be greater than 5cm. Cut out the circle and draw a line from its centre to its edge.

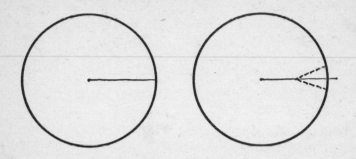

5. Cut the V-shaped notch from the edge to about halfway along the line you have just drawn.

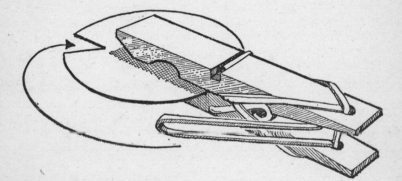

6. Place the cardboard disc into the mouth of the clothes peg so that the notch is facing away from the peg. Stretch the rubber band loop around and into the notch.

7. Hold the clothes peg as shown. (It can be completely hidden from onlookers behind your hand, which adds to the effect.) Press gently and the flying saucer will spin up and away.

8. With paints or ink markers, try drawing coloured spots on your flying saucer. When in flight these spots will appear to change into circles and may even, apparently, change colour.

If you paint red and blue spots on white card as shown – red, blue, blue, red from top to bottom – you will get red, white and blue circles when the saucer spins. If you paint them red, blue, red, blue, you will get two purple circles.

If you paint half the disc one colour and the other half another colour, when in flight the saucer will appear to be yet a third colour.

Shoe box 'guitar'

You will need: *five thin rubber bands*
one shoe box
scissors
pencil and ruler

1. Make vertical cuts in the middle, and at one end, of the long sides of the shoe box. Then flatten the pieces out.

2. Make five little cuts in the top of each side. These should be about 0.5cm deep and about 1.5cm apart, starting from the remaining end of the box. Fold the two flattened sides in half towards the bottom of the box.

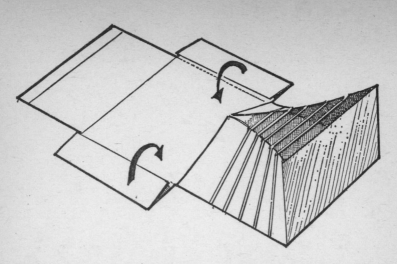

3. Fold the sides into the box. (The cardboard will not lie very flat but that does not matter.)

4. Stretch the rubber bands around the box, fitting them into the cuts at the top of the sides. The box will automatically change its shape as the standing ends come together.

5. Make two more cuts as shown and fold the sides in again to form a handle.

6. The completed 'guitar'. Place it on your lap, pluck the strings and see if you can play a tune.

Sealed box mystery

This is an impressive trick which is not difficult to perform once you have made the necessary apparatus.

You will need:
*three thin rubber bands
one empty matchbox
scrap of cotton cloth
needle and thread
scrap of tin
craft knife and old scissors
pencil and ruler*

1.   To make a little bag – prepare a rectangle of cloth 10 × 16cm. Fold the two shorter edges together.

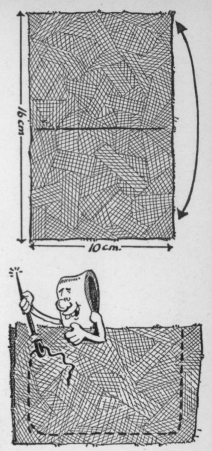

2.   Stitch about 1cm from the sides. Curve neatly at the bottom corners and fasten the ends well. Turn inside out and fold the top edge inwards, stitching it in place.

3.   This is the bag completed.

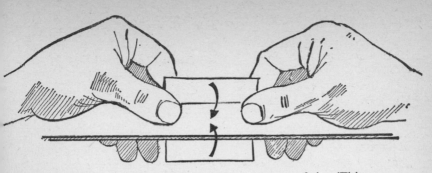

4. To make a chute – prepare a 5.5cm square of tin. (This can be done by cutting the square from the side of a tin can after removing the top and bottom with a craft knife and flattening the side.) Take care not to cut yourself. It is easiest to score the lines first with a craft knife and then to cut out the shape with an old pair of scissors.

Place a ruler across the centre of the tin square and bend the top and bottom around the ruler. Remove the ruler and continue to shape the chute if necessary.

5. The completed chute.

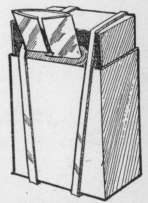

6. Place the chute in the bag. Fold the sides of the bag over neatly and twist a rubber band around it a few times.

7. Place the bag in the matchbox. The chute will stick out at the top. Twist a couple of rubber bands around the box lengthways.

Slip this apparatus into a side pocket of your jacket and you are ready to provide your friends with a real puzzle at any time.

When you have gathered an audience about you, ask to borrow a 5p piece, and get the owner to mark it in some way so that he will be sure to recognise it again.

Hold the coin between thumb and finger and drop it into your pocket, making a few magic passes with your other hand as you do so. Try not to put your hand into your pocket, just your thumb and forefinger. (Secretly you drop the coin through the chute, then quickly remove the chute from the box, leaving both in your pocket. When the chute is removed, all the rubber bands contract and thereby seal the box.)

After an interval, during which you can perform some other trick, put your hand in your pocket and take out the matchbox. With your thumb, secretly slide the surrounding rubber bands to a more central position. Put the box before the person whose 5p piece you borrowed and ask him to open it. After removing the rubber bands, opening the box, taking out the little bag and removing the band from that, he will be astonished to find his 5p piece inside.

56

PART 3

THINGS TO MAKE
USING RUBBER BANDS
AND CRAFT MATERIALS

Harpoon

You will need: *two thin rubber bands*
one stick, about 30cm long (a
length of balsa is easiest to work
with)
craft knife
bradawl

1. Shape one end of the
stick with the craft knife to
give it a sloping edge. Using
the bradawl, make a hole
through the stick about 1cm
from the other end.

2. Cut out a wedge shape
behind the pointed end. Push
a rubber band through the
hole and loop it over itself.

3. Tie the second rubber
band to the first as shown on
page 28.

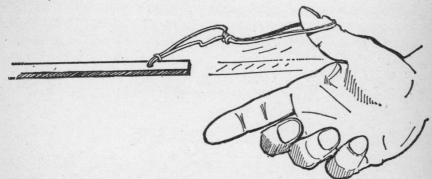

4. The harpoon is now ready for use. Place your thumb through the loop and grip the pointed end. Aim at the target and release the harpoon.

5. The harpoon will leap forward, but your thumb through the loop prevents it from getting away from you completely. It remains ready to hand for firing again.

Fish targets for harpooning

In some parts of the world people use harpoons very much like the one on the previous page for catching fish from streams and shallow rivers. Here is a way to make fish targets so that you can test your skill with a harpoon.

You will need : *drawing paper or thin card*
pencil
scissors or craft knife
hair pins or paper clips
adhesive tape

1. Prepare rectangles of paper or card measuring about 10 × 25cm and fold the shorter sides together. Place the folded edge at the top and draw a full round fish shape.

2. Cut around your drawing but not along the folded edge. Turn over.

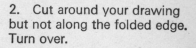

3. Take a hairpin, or paper clip, and shape it so that it becomes wide enough to receive the harpoon. Then fix the pin to the target with adhesive tape.

4. Make several fish in this way, then stand them up and catch them by firing your harpoon at them.

When this becomes too easy, you can attach a long thread to one of the fish, and take it in turns with a friend to pull it slowly across the floor while the other one tries to catch it.

Letter rack

You will need : *thirty-six thin rubber bands*
sheet of thick card (e.g.
mounting card)
craft knife
glue
pencil and ruler

1. Cut out six 15 × 20cm rectangles of card. Find the centre of each side of one of the rectangles and make cuts of about 0.5cm as shown – that is to say, make a 0.5cm cut in each corner and two cuts at the centre of each side.

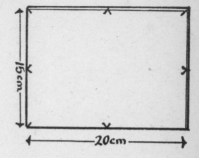

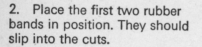

2. Place the first two rubber bands in position. They should slip into the cuts.

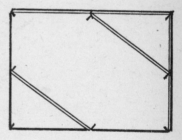

3. The third rubber band lies diagonally across the first two.

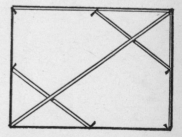

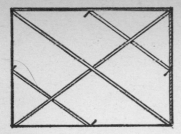

4. Place the fourth band in the other diagonal position.

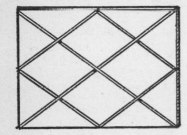

5. Place a band across the top left and bottom right corners. This completes one section. Do the same with the other five rectangles.

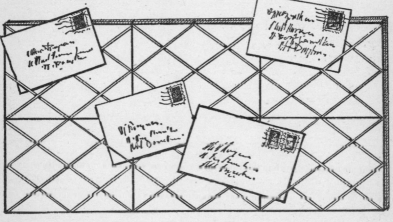

6. Cut a 30 × 60cm sheet of card and glue the six sections to it to complete the rack.

This would be fun to have in your own room to hold letters and cards, or you could make a family size one by adding more sections and give it to your parents to hang up in the hall.

Bat and ball

You will need:

five or six thin rubber bands
sheet of balsa, about
0.25cm thick
thick card (e.g. mounting card)
table tennis ball
compasses
needle and thread
craft knife or scissors
glue
pencil and ruler
bradawl (pointed scissors
will do)

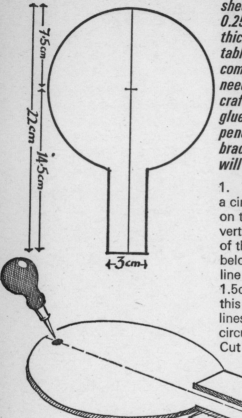

1. To make a bat shape, draw a circle with a radius of 7.5cm on the card, then draw a vertical line through the centre of the circle. Measure 14.5cm below the centre along this line and mark a distance of 1.5cm to the right and left of this point. Then draw vertical lines from there to the circumference of the circle. Cut out this shape.

2. Cut out two rectangles of balsa measuring 3×10cm. Glue these to the top and bottom of the card so that the ends are flush. This forms the handle.

Make a hole about 1cm from the circumference at the opposite end.

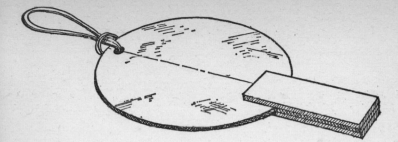

3. Push a rubber band through this hole and loop it on to itself. Add four or five more bands (as shown on page 28).

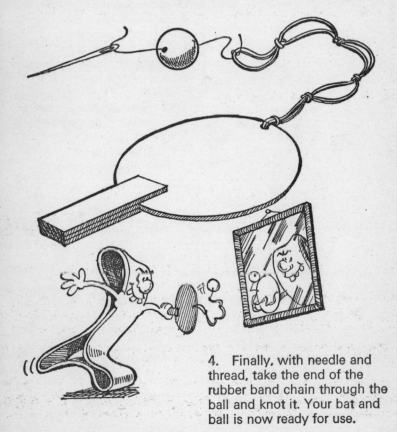

4. Finally, with needle and thread, take the end of the rubber band chain through the ball and knot it. Your bat and ball is now ready for use.

'Smiley card'
You will need:

one thin rubber band
drawing paper
scissors or craft knife
adhesive tape
glue
pencil and ruler
ink markers or paints for
decoration

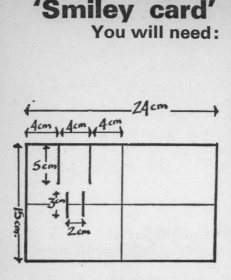

1. Prepare a rectangle of drawing paper 15 × 24cm. Fold the edges together and crease the centre lines. Open up.

At the top left, draw two vertical lines 5cm long and 4cm apart.

Below and between these, with the horizontal crease as their centre, draw two vertical lines 3cm long and 2cm apart.

Cut along these four lines and turn the paper over.

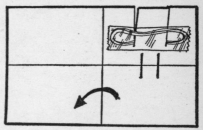

2. Place the rubber band over the tongue of paper and slide it down as far as it will go. Fix the rubber band in position with adhesive tape.

Having done this, fold the paper in half from right to left and glue the two layers lightly together.

3. Draw a face around the rubber band, treating the band as a mouth.

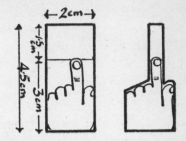

4. Prepare a piece of paper 2×4.5cm. Measure 3cm from the bottom and, in the area below this, draw a hand as shown. Make it fill up the space.

Cut around the hand but continue the cuts on either side of the pointing finger up to the top edge.

5. Half close the card with the face inside, pulling forward the little strip at the centre so that it stands out.

Take the hand and bend it at the fingertip. Hook the finger over the rubber band and, using just a spot of glue, fix it to the back of the hand. Glue the base of the hand to the vertical part of the centre strip.

67

6. Close the card and write a suitable message on the front.

7. When the card is opened, the paper finger will pull the rubber band mouth into a shy smile. Finish off the drawing by adding an arm to the hand and decorate with colour.

Valentine card

You will need : *one thin rubber band*
drawing paper
scissors or craft knife
adhesive tape
glue
pencil and ruler
ink markers or paints for
decoration

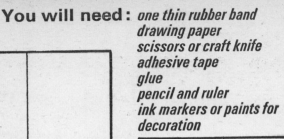

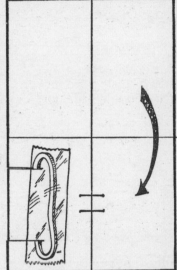

1. Prepare a rectangle of
paper 15 × 24cm. Fold the
edges together and crease
the centre lines. Open up.

From the bottom right
corner, measure up 3cm and
then a further 6cm. Draw
horizontal lines, 3cm long,
from these two points.

With the vertical crease as
their centre, draw two
horizontal lines, 2cm long and
1.5cm apart between the two
lines you have already drawn.

Cut along these four lines
and turn the paper over.

2. Place the rubber band on
to the tongue of paper and
slide it across as far as it will
go. Fix the band in position
with adhesive tape.

Now fold the top edge to the
bottom edge and glue the two
layers together. Turn over.

69

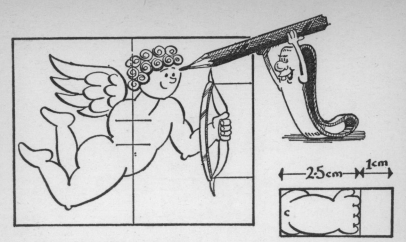

3. Make a drawing of Cupid as shown, treating the rubber band as the string of Cupid's bow.

4. Prepare a piece of paper 1.5 × 3.5cm. Measure 2.5cm from the left and draw Cupid's arm within this area.

5. Half close the card, pulling forward the little strip at the centre so that it stands out.

Bend back the end flap on the arm piece; hook it on to the rubber band and glue the shoulder to the centre strip.

6. Close the card and write your message on the front.

7. When the card is opened, Cupid will pull the bow string and release it with a 'twang'.

Rubber band motor 1

You will need : *one thin rubber band
one empty cotton reel
matchstick
piece of candle
cocktail stick (or similar)
adhesive tape
knife*

1. Push the rubber band through the cotton reel.

2. Cut a matchstick in half and slip this through one end of the band. Pull the other end of the band tight so that the stick is held firmly in place.

3. Stick adhesive tape to the matchstick end of the cotton reel.
    Cut about 1cm from the end of a candle and hollow out the centre to make a wax washer. Slip this over the remaining end of the rubber band.

4. Place a cocktail stick (or something similar) through the rubber band and wind it up.

This completes the basic rubber band motor. Place it on a smooth surface and it will run forward. See the following pages for a way of using this motor.

Running duck

You will need : *one rubber band motor no. 1 (see page 72)*
drawing paper or thin card
pencil and ruler
craft knife or scissors
glue
ink markers or paints for decoration

1.   Prepare a rectangle of paper or card, 15 ×16cm. Mark off the measurements as shown and draw the four horizontal lines.
   Make the two cuts at the left. Then fold the card in half on the centre line.
2.   Cut a full, curved line from the top right corner to the centre bottom of the folded card, then open it up.

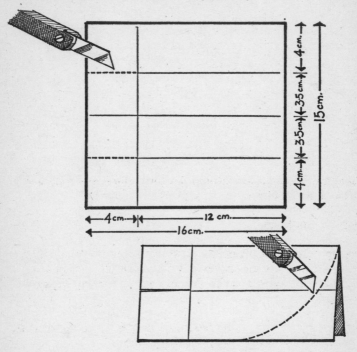

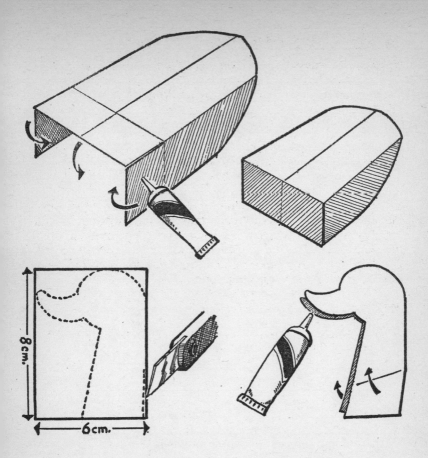

3. Close the front end by folding the three flaps together and gluing them in place.

4. Step 3 completed.

5. Prepare a piece of paper, 8 × 12cm, and fold the two shorter edges together. Draw the shape of a duck's head and neck as shown. Then cut the shape out, but cut only part way up the folded edge.

6. Join the two layers of the beak together with a spot of glue. Bend up the lower part of the neck at an angle.

7.   Glue the head section to the body. Give your duck some eyes and add further decoration.

8.   Stand the duck on a smooth surface. Wind up your rubber band motor and place it just behind him. The motor will run forward into the duck – and off he goes.

Rubber band motor 2

You will need:

four thin rubber bands
sheet of balsa, about 0.25cm thick
sheet of balsa, about 1cm thick
two cotton reels
four panel pins
thick card (e.g. mounting card)
pair of pliers
glue
pencil and ruler
craft knife
pair of compasses

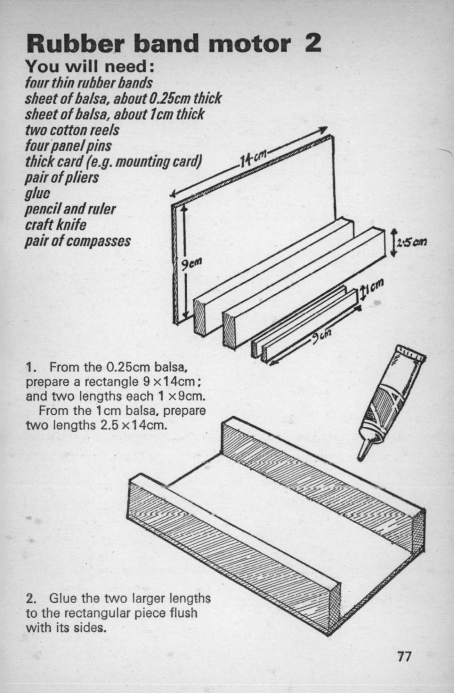

1. From the 0.25cm balsa, prepare a rectangle 9×14cm; and two lengths each 1×9cm.
   From the 1cm balsa, prepare two lengths 2.5×14cm.

2. Glue the two larger lengths to the rectangular piece flush with its sides.

3. Measure and mark 4cm from each end of these two pieces. Bend the heads of all four panel pins with a pair of pliers. Push one into each of these four points so that the heads face outwards.

Glue the remaining two balsa strips across the ends.

4. Remove the paper from the ends of the cotton reels and insert a rubber band through each of two opposite apertures.

5. Cut out four discs from thick card, each with a radius of 2.2cm. Cut a circular hole with a radius of 0.7cm in the centre of each disc, and glue one disc on each end of each cotton reel, allowing the ends of the rubber bands to poke through the centre holes of the discs.

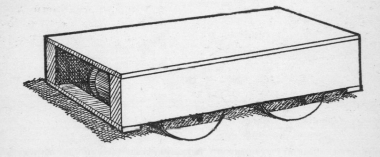

6. Put one twist at each end of the rubber bands – i.e. treating each pair of bands as one – and hook each end of the rubber bands on to a panel pin . . .

7. . . . and turn over.

To operate, place the motor on the floor or a table and keep hold of it while you run it back along the surface; this will wind up the rubber bands. Release the motor and it will run forward automatically.

See the next project for a way of building on to this motor.

Steam engine

You will need: *one rubber band motor no. 2*
one tin can
one small cardboard box
paper
glue and adhesive tape
craft knife or scissors
ink markers or paints for
decoration

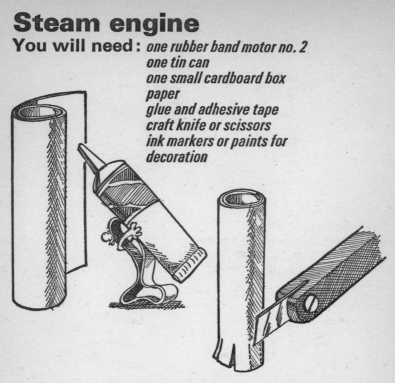

1.   To make a chimney, cut the paper into a rectangle about 8 × 16cm. Roll it into a tube and glue.

2.   Cut slits in one end.

3.   Cut rectangular shapes from two sides of the cardboard box and let this serve as the engine driver's cabin, as shown in the diagram. The tin can forms the boiler. Fold up the cut ends of the chimney and stick them to the boiler. When you have everything in position on the base (you may find parts stick out over the edges) fix them together with adhesive tape or glue. Decorate with ink markers or paints.
By running the motor back and then releasing it, as described on page 79, your steam engine will race forwards realistically. The design could be modified to produce a car or other wheeled vehicle.

Creepy-crawly

You will need:

two thin rubber bands
one empty cotton reel
wire (coat hanger)
adhesive tape
craft knife or scissors
thin card and paper
pair of pliers
pair of compasses
2m of strong thread
pencil and ruler
ink markers or paints for
decoration
glue
thick card (e.g. mounting card)

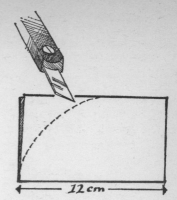

1. To make the creepy-crawly's head: cut a 12cm square from the thin card. Fold this in half and draw a full curve from the left of the folded edge to about halfway up the opposite side. Cut along this line.

2. Cut a 16cm length of wire from an old coat hanger (this can be done without wire cutters by cutting around the wire with a craft knife until it is thin enough to snap).

Make hooks at each end of the wire with pliers; then make an angle at the centre of the wire so that the hooks lie about 8cm apart.

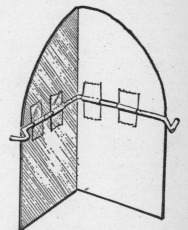

3. Fix the wire to the card across its centre. This can best be done by fixing short strips of adhesive tape across the wire.

4. Now fix adhesive tape along the length of the wire. Make a hole just below the wire (with scissors, or a bradawl).

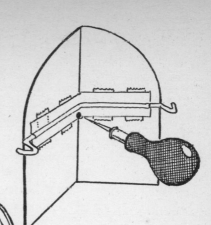

5. Remove the labels from the cotton reel and insert a rubber band through each of two opposite apertures.

6. Cut two discs from thick card, each with a radius of 2.2cm. Cut a circular hole with a radius of 0.7cm in the centre of each disc. Glue the discs on each end of the reel, allowing the rubber bands to poke through the centre holes of the discs.

4·4cm

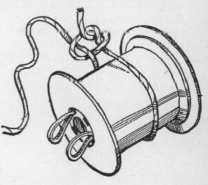

7. Tie one end of the thread firmly to the reel with a slip knot. Pull tight. (If this knot is not tight the mechanism may not work properly.)

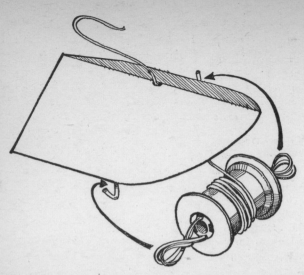

8. Wind the greater part of the thread on to the reel, allowing the end of the thread to pass through the hole in the card.
    Make one twist in either end of each band and hook on to the wire.

9. Tie the end of the thread to a rubber band or curtain ring. This completes the head and working part of the creepy-crawly. Decorate with ink markers or paints.

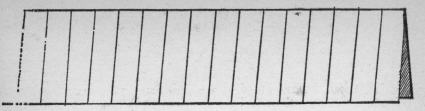

10. To make the creepy-crawly's body: prepare a strip of paper 12cm wide and almost any length. (Try to find some wrapping paper with a suitable pattern or colour.)

Fold the two longer edges together; then pleat, making each fold about 1.5cm apart.

11. Hold one end of the pleated strip as shown and pull the two layers apart. The crease at the top will spread to form a new, triangular crease. Press this firmly into place.

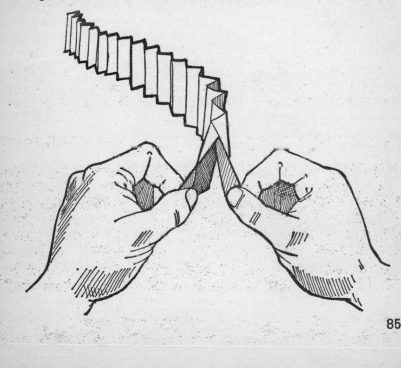

12. Holding the tops of the first and second pleats between the thumb and forefinger of each hand, pull them apart. The paper will spread and form a new crease along the top, which should be pressed firmly into place. Continue with the next pair of pleats, and so on along the length of the strip until it resembles the drawing in fig. 12.

13. Glue the body to the head and the creepy-crawly is completed. With your finger through the end loop, allow him to drop to the floor (this will have the effect of winding up the rubber band) and he will run forward. You can walk along, pulling on the thread occasionally, and the creepy-crawly will run along beside you, his body contracting and expanding in a most amusing way.

Paddle boat

You will need:

two thin rubber bands
sheet of balsa, about
0.23cm thick
length of balsa, 1.25cm square
used matchstick
pencil and ruler
craft knife
bradawl
60° set square
needle and thread
glue
extras for decoration

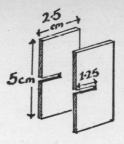

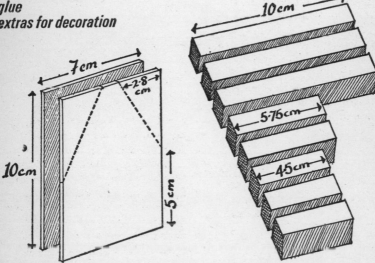

1. Cut the 1.25cm square balsa into three 10cm lengths ; two 5.75cm lengths ; three 4.5cm lengths.

From the 0.25cm sheet cut two 7×10cm pieces and two 2.5×5cm pieces. Then cut the larger pieces as shown ; the cuts are from points 5cm up the longer sides to points 2.8cm in from the top corners.

At left centre of the smaller pieces, cut a 1.25cm slit, 0.25cm wide.

2. Bore a hole in each of two of the 10cm lengths, 1.25cm from one end. Assemble these two pieces with two of the 4.5cm pieces and one of the sheets as shown. Glue together.

3. Take the remaining 10cm length and the two 5.75cm lengths and on each of them mark a 30° angle at one end and a 60° angle at the other. Cut away the corners.

4. Assemble the two small sheets to form the paddle. Place the two rubber bands around it as shown.

5. Tie thread around the bands on either side of the paddle and use another piece of thread to pull the ends of the bands through the holes.

Continue forming the boat by gluing the remaining 4.5cm length at centre front and the two short-angled pieces on either side of it.

6. Glue the remaining two
pieces, the deck and keel, to
the top and bottom of the
boat. Cut a matchstick in two;
place one piece in each end
of the rubber band protruding
from the paddle, and tighten.

7. The paddle boat completed.
You may add a matchbox and
a piece of dowelling (or a
pencil stub) to make a bridge
and funnel.

Wind up the paddle. Put the
boat in a bath of water and
watch it go.

Rapid rubber band repeater

You will need : *several thin rubber bands*
sheet of hard quality
balsa, 0.25cm thick
craft knife
pencil and ruler
60° set square
glue

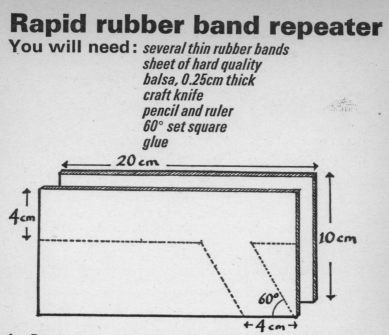

1.   Prepare two rectangles of balsa, 10×20cm. Measure down 4cm from the top and draw a horizontal line. Draw a line 60° to the bottom right corner and another at 4cm to the left of that. Cut out this shape. Save the scraps ; you will need them later on in this project.

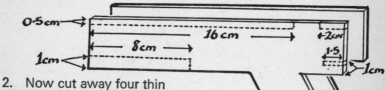

2.   Now cut away four thin rectangular pieces from each sheet : at top left, a 0.5×16cm area ; at top right, a 0.5×2cm piece ; at bottom left, an area 1×8cm ; all must be removed. At bottom right, measure up 1cm and *below* this point make a slit 0.2×1.5cm.

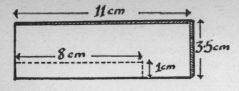

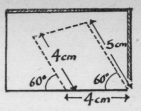

3. From a scrap of balsa, prepare a rectangle 3.5 × 11cm. Cut a 1 × 8cm area from the bottom left corner.

4. On another scrap of balsa, draw two lines at 60° to the edge, 4cm apart. Mark one of these lines 4cm long and the other 5cm long. Draw a line to connect these two points and cut out the shape.

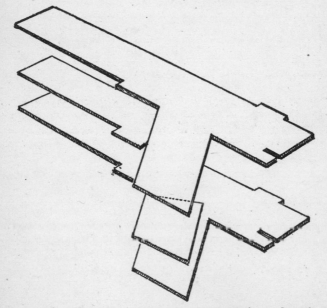

5. Now glue together the pieces you have made so far: the two pieces completed in step 2 go above and below the pieces made in steps 3 and 4. Make sure that the step 3 piece is flush with the front of the barrel, and the step 4 piece flush with the heel of the butt.

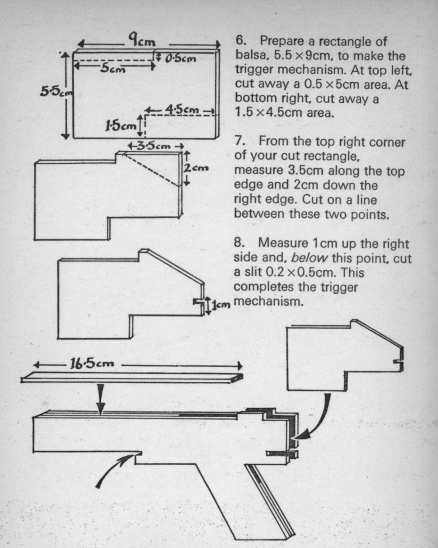

6. Prepare a rectangle of balsa, 5.5 × 9cm, to make the trigger mechanism. At top left, cut away a 0.5 × 5cm area. At bottom right, cut away a 1.5 × 4.5cm area.

7. From the top right corner of your cut rectangle, measure 3.5cm along the top edge and 2cm down the right edge. Cut on a line between these two points.

8. Measure 1cm up the right side and, *below* this point, cut a slit 0.2 × 0.5cm. This completes the trigger mechanism.

9. Prepare a strip of balsa 0.75 × 16.5cm. Glue this to the top of the pistol. One end should be flush against the rear top projections and the other end should stick out at the front.

Make a cut, 0.2 × 0.5cm, just below the barrel at the point indicated with an arrow-head.

Now slip the trigger mechanism into the back of the pistol.

10. Stretch a rubber band around the pistol and into the slits below the barrel and at the back. This will act as a spring for the trigger mechanism.

Stretch two or three more bands around the length of the pistol. These serve as your ammunition. Squeeze the trigger gently backwards and upwards and the rubber bands will shoot off one at a time; as one is released another moves up to take its place.

If you make paper targets for your repeater, the bands will hit them with a loud 'thwack'.

More Beaver Books

We hope you have enjoyed this Beaver Book. Here are some of the other titles:

The Beaver Book of Games George and Cornelia Kay describe dozens of games to play indoors and outdoors, including all the old favourites plus lots of new ones. Illustrated by Robin Anderson

What's the Answer A mixed bag of puzzles using numbers, words and pictures; all fun to try. A Beaver original

Pleasure Trove A collection of stories, poems, limericks, jokes, riddles and things to make and do by Jennifer Curry

The Beaver Book of Brain Ticklers A Beaver original. Intriguing puzzles and teasers of a mathematical type invented by Charles Booth-Jones; illustrated with cartoons, diagrams and line drawings

Picture Puzzles Ninety-six pages packed with a variety of brain-teasers, including mazes, 'spot-the-difference' and 'I spy' games, written and illustrated by Walter Shepherd

Animal Quiz Johnny Morris, universally known and loved for his television programme Animal Magic, has created a picture quiz book about all sorts of animals, fish and birds, full of fun and fact for all the family

New Beavers are published every month and if you would like the *Beaver Bulletin* – which gives all the details – please send a stamped addressed envelope to:

Beaver Bulletin
The Hamlyn Group
Astronaut House
Feltham
Middlesex TW14 9AR

387534